AMERICAN HORTICULTURAL SOCIETY
PRACTICAL GUIDES

FUCHSIAS

AMERICAN HORTICULTURAL SOCIETY
PRACTICAL GUIDES

FUCHSIAS

GEORGE BARTLETT

DORLING KINDERSLEY PUBLISHING, INC.
www.dk.com

EG
VK LE PH DP TS [DK] VK HC CADCC MA
C TL PR

DORLING KINDERSLEY PUBLISHING, INC. RW VK
www.dk.com

PROJECT EDITOR Simon Maughan
SERIES EDITOR Gillian Roberts
SERIES ART EDITOR Stephen Josland

SENIOR MANAGING EDITOR Mary-Clare Jerram
SENIOR MANAGING ART EDITOR Lee Griffiths

US CONSULTANTS Al Sydnor, Elsie Sydnor
US EDITOR Ray Rogers

DTP DESIGNER Louise Paddick
PRODUCTION Mandy Inness

First American Edition, 2000
2 4 6 8 10 9 7 5 3 1

Published in the United States by
Dorling Kindersley Publishing, Inc., 95 Madison Avenue, New York, NY 10016

Dorling Kindersley Publishing offers special discounts for bulk purchases for sales
promotions or premiums. Specific, large-quantity needs can be met with special editions,
including personalized covers, excerpts of existing guides, and corporate imprints. For
more information, contact Special Markets Department, Dorling Kindersley Publishing,
Inc., 95 Madison Avenue, New York, NY 10016 Fax: 800-600-9098

Library of Congress Cataloging-in-Publication Data
Fuchsias.
    p. cm — (AHS practical guides)
    ISBN 0-7894-5068-2 (pbk. : alk. paper)
    1. Fuchsias. I. Dorling Kindersley Publishing, Inc. II. American
Horticultural Society. III. Series
    SB413.F8F837 2000
    635.9'3376—dc21   99-41068
                                                        CIP

Reproduced by Colourscan, Singapore
Printed and bound by Star Standard Industries, Singapore

CONTENTS

GETTING TO KNOW FUCHSIAS

WHAT ARE FUCHSIAS?

WITH THE SIMPLICITY of their pendulous flowers and the ease with which they can be grown, fuchsias are extremely popular plants. They are also truly versatile, from low creepers suitable as groundcovers to fuchsias that can be trained and clipped into a wide range of shapes. In milder climates, which are favored by fuchsias, some will grow as large hedges or small trees.

A BRIEF HISTORY OF FUCHSIAS

The majority of wild fuchsias are found in the lower wooded foothills of Central and South America, and they became known to the modern world only in 1703, when *Fuchsia triphylla flore coccinea* was discovered by Father Charles Plumier. The name *Fuchsia* was given to honor the German botanist, Leonard Fuchs. The first plants were grown in Europe in the early 1790s, but hybridization did not begin until 1825; it is from those very early crosses that we have such a wealth of color and form available to us today. Considerable progress continues to be made, and some of the results have been magnificent.

FUCHSIAS GIVE FAST RESULTS

Perhaps one of the most satisfying aspects of fuchsias is their speedy growth. Young plants purchased or rooted in early spring will dramatically develop into flowering plants by early summer. Fuchsias that permanently reside in garden borders will grow tall new flowering stems from their root systems within just a few months.

◄ HANGING BLOOM
Fuchsias are famous for their pendulous flowers. These blooms belong to a bush fuchsia called 'Lye's Unique', which continues to be very popular, even though it was introduced over one hundred years ago.

◄ IN FULL GLORY *'Blush of Dawn' is a fully double fuchsia suitable for a hanging container.*

TYPES OF FUCHSIA

As soon as horticulturists were able to grow fuchsias successfully, hybridization began in earnest. Beautiful new cultivars became available, and today we have fuchsias for many garden uses, all with their unmistakable and colorful flowers. Bush fuchsias, trailing fuchsias, and fuchsias grown as standards are the main categories of interest, but the diversity is great, so it is worth taking a deeper look.

WHAT ARE SPECIES FUCHSIAS?

Fuchsias that grow wild in their native habitats are known as Species fuchsias. Most of this group have reddish flowers

> **Species fuchsias are the ancestors of all the modern cultivars**

with long thin tubes and trumpet-shaped sepals and petals. There is a reason for this shape and color; they attract hummingbirds, which pollinate the flowers.

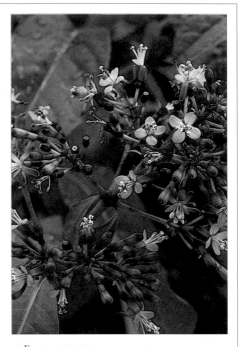

▲ *F. PANICULATA*
Known as "the lilac fuchsia" for its large bunches of very small flowers, this plant has very strong, upright growth, which makes it easy to grow – a good choice for a beginner.

▲ *F. MICROPHYLLA*
Like other Encliandra fuchsias (see facing page), this one has beautiful small flowers. It also has fernlike and delicate foliage.

▲ 'LOXENSIS'
Although given a cultivar name, this fuchsia is a hybrid between two Species fuchsias. It has upright and bushy, rampant growth.

F. PROCUMBENS
This is a popular
and easy fuchsia to
grow in a hanging
container. The
trailing growth is
very attractive.

SPECIES FUCHSIAS TO GROW

There are more than one hundred Species fuchsias so far identified, although only a handful of these are available to gardeners. Specialist fuchsia nurseries are the best places to seek them out.

F. *magellanica* is without doubt the most popular Species fuchsia in cultivation. A considerable number of variants exist, and F. *magellanica* 'Versicolor', with its white and silvery pink leaf markings, is among the best. They are all very easy to grow and hardy to USDA Zone 6.

F. *procumbens* merits special attention: its upward-looking flowers make it unique. They are like miniature golden goblets with green sepals and blue pollen – colors very rarely found in fuchsias. The fruit, when they form, should be left on the plant; they are also attractive, being much larger than the small flowers.

ENCLIANDRA FUCHSIAS

A collection of fuchsias belonging to the Encliandra group will provide considerable interest. They are characterized by their small foliage and flowers, and long wiry stems, which are easily twined around wire shapes to produce interesting structures (*see pp.44–47*). F. *microphylla* subsp. *hidalgensis*, with white flowers, is ideal for this kind of topiary work. Scent is very rare for fuchsias, but a delicate perfume can be found in the extraordinary flowers of 'Neopolitan', which are white, maturing to red through pink; all three colors may be present at once.

RECOMMENDED SPECIES FUCHSIAS

F. *arborescens* Bunches of lilac-blue flowers.

F. *boliviana* Rose-red flowers with long, slender tubes and backward-curving sepals.

F. *denticulata* Long-tubed, dark red flowers with bright orange petals. Easy to grow.

F. *fulgens* Long, trumpet-shaped orange flowers. Several varieties.

F. *glazioviana* Small flowers with red sepals and a violet corolla. A strong and easy grower.

F. *magellanica* Many varieties exist in cultivation, all with variations in flower and foliage color. Quite hardy and easy to grow.

F. *microphylla* subsp. *hidalgensis* White flowers on wiry, spreading growth.

F. *paniculata* Lilac flowers and laurel-like foliage. Its vigor makes it easy to grow.

F. *procumbens* Small, upward-looking flowers on a creeping plant. Good for a beginner.

F. *venusta* Long and thin, carmine-red flowers. Strong, spreading growth; best in a large pot.

RECOGNIZING FUCHSIA FLOWER SHAPES

VARIETY AND DIVISIONS
Fuchsia flowers are usually tubular and hanging. Single flowers have four petals, semidouble flowers have between five and seven, and fully double flowers have eight or more. The petals as a group are called the corolla.

Stamens · Ovary · Sepals · Petals · Tube · Stigma

F. PROCUMBENS   SINGLE   SEMIDOUBLE   DOUBLE   TRIPHYLLA TYPE

FUCHSIA FLOWER SHAPES

The legacy of over two centuries of fuchsia breeding gives the modern gardener a wide array of flowers to choose from. Fuchsia flowers are almost always pendulous. They vary from very large to quite small, and they are borne more or less continuously through summer and autumn. Three main divisions exist – single, semidouble, and double – which are based on the number of petals a flower has. The diagrams above show the anatomy of typical fuchsia flowers.

The fuchsia cultivars known as Triphyllas have long-tubed flowers with trumpet-shaped sepals and petals, and it is this distinctive characteristic that sets them apart from the rest. Those of *F. procumbens* point upward.

▲ 'CITATION'
The backward-curving sepals on these single flowers expose the four white petals.

▲ 'PIPPA'
This semidouble cultivar has bright flowers with between five and seven petals.

▲ 'DARK EYES'
The numerous petals of this double-flowered bush fuchsia are tightly rolled at the center.

VERSATILE GROWTH

• The vigorous growth of fuchsias is easily trained into different shapes (*see pp.44–47*).
• A standard fuchsia is really a trailing or a bush cultivar made to grow with a very long, bare stem that branches only at the top.

BUSH AND TRAILING FUCHSIAS

When you read a description of a fuchsia in a nursery catalog, the plant will usually be described as either a bush or a trailer.

The growth of bush fuchsias is further divided into upright or lax. Without doubt, the strong, upright growers will make the best bush fuchsias with little effort on your part. Those with lax growth, such as 'Swingtime', are best in hanging baskets or containers, although the growth is perhaps a little too stiff to trail naturally.

Trailing fuchsias have very lax growth, which naturally cascades over the edge of containers or walls, with flowers borne at the ends of the trails. Properly raised, they give a lot of color. The finest standards are produced from trailing fuchsias, although bush types with strong, upright growth may be easier for the beginner.

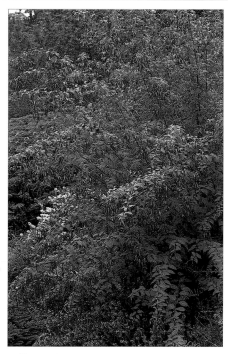

▲ *F. MAGELLANICA*
The strong, upright growth of this bush fuchsia makes it suitable for use in a border. Where hardy, it can be left outside and clipped as a hedge.

▲ 'CORALLINA'
The rather lax, spreading growth of this bush looks good trailing over a wall.

◄ 'TOM THUMB'
Classed as an upright bush, this small cultivar grows to only about 12in (30cm) tall.

THE COLOR RANGE

T HE DELICATE APPEARANCE of the fuchsia flower is enhanced by the attractive color combinations produced by the tube, sepals, and corolla. A wide selection of the spectrum is available, with the exception of pure yellow and true blue, from the purest of whites right through to very dark purple or near black. Perhaps the most popular fuchsias are those with delicate pastel shading.

MULTICOLORED FLOWERS

Perhaps it is the contrast or delicate variation between the colors of the sepals and corolla that gives fuchsias their greatest appeal. Some double-flowered cultivars even show color contrast within the corolla, which gives rise to well-chosen names such as 'Peppermint Stick', although a simple description hardly does full justice

to this large-flowered fuchsia with striped tubes and multicoloured petals. The bold shading of 'Joy Patmore', with its pure waxy white sepals and rich carmine-pink corolla, also demands attention. Another extremely striking color combination is seen in 'Celia Smedley', whose pale rose-pink tube and sepals serve to enhance the vivid red coloring of the corolla.

THE FUCHSIA SPECTRUM
With over 8,000 different fuchsias in cultivation, small wonder that there are colors to suit all tastes and moods. The enormous variation is incredible, from simple whites to frivolous pinks, and bright reds to somber purples. It is often the particular size or shape of a flower, or the way in which it is carried, that can give a particular bloom its distinguishing features.

'SNOW WHITE'

'LEONORA'

'ANNABEL'

'ARABELLA'

'ALICE HOFFMAN'

SINGLE-COLORED FLOWERS

Occasionally, all parts of the flower are exactly the same color. Such flowers are usually referred to as "self-colored," and there are many wonderful examples, like Turkey red 'Rufus', which has coloring so bright that it appears to glow. Most Triphylla fuchsias have flowers of just a single color, and they are all very attractive, especially bright crimson 'Mary', which stands out like a beacon. A white Triphylla, 'Our Ted', has also been produced.

Many of the fuchsias with all-white flowers, however, tend to have less appeal as the white often takes on a slight grayish look with maturity, and they are easily bruised. Despite this, there is one white-flowered fuchsia that is far superior to any other; it is called 'Hawkshead' and is well worth seeking out.

If you are looking for the elusive yellow, try the unusual *F. procumbens*, which has that color in small quantities. The realization of an all-yellow cultivar, however, continues to elude discovery.

TRADITIONAL FUCHSIA COLORS

The colors that are still recognized as true fuchsia, the reds and the purples, are seen at their very best in some of the larger, double-flowered cultivars, like 'Royal Velvet'. Many have purple corollas of the deepest hue, and in 'Gruss aus dem Bodethal' they verge on black. Even with this somber coloring, the plants are extremely attractive.

'CORALLE'

'JACK SHAHAN'

'MARY'

'LA ROSITA'

'FEY'

'CECILE'

FUCHSIAS FOR FOLIAGE

O NE WOULD THINK that the great diversity of color, shape, and size seen among fuchsia flowers would be riches enough; but there are also several fuchsias that produce delightful shades in the foliage, variegated or plain. Although these plants will (being fuchsias) continue to produce flowers as well, the beauty of foliage fuchsias sometimes comes into its own when both these elements combine.

THE RANGE OF FUCHSIA FOLIAGE

Quite a number of fuchsias are blessed with extremely attractive foliage; some have leaves that are golden green, while many others have variegated patterns enhanced with different colors and contrasting veins. Even some of the hardy *F. magellanica* fuchsias display foliage color variations. There are the golden yellow leaves of *F. magellanica* var. *gracilis* 'Aurea' and the distinctive cream, green, and pink variegation of *F. magellanica* var. *gracilis* 'Variegata', for example. When this group of fuchsias is allowed to grow in an open garden or as a hedge, the plants will produce both the delightful foliage and also an abundant supply of flowers.

Because the color of the foliage is visible even in young plants, choosing a fuchsia for its foliage when you are at a nursery is far easier than choosing for the flowers, since it is possible to see exactly what you are about to buy.

DISPLAYING THE FOLIAGE

Foliage plays a major role when it comes to the coordination of color schemes. In the border, fuchsias of the Triphylla type, especially if grown as standards, add both height and color to any display. Most Triphylla fuchsias have a delightful purple sheen on the undersides of the leaves, which will be subtly revealed in the slightest of breezes.

TRAILS OF COLOR
The growth of 'Autumnale' is quite horizontal, which makes this plant an interesting choice for a hanging container. The young leaves start out green and yellow then age to dark red, salmon, and yellow.

◀ A FLORAL MATCH
'Golden Marinka'
produces beautifully
variegated foliage as
well as an abundance
of flowers. It is a
trailing cultivar and
it will quickly fill a
container with color.

▼ 'TOM WEST'
The young leaves
have the best color, so
pinch out the growing
tips (see p.46).

Within hanging containers, the bonus of colored foliage cannot be over emphasized. It is possible to grow superb hanging containers filled entirely with a single fuchsia cultivar with remarkable foliage. 'Autumnale', with its stiff horizontal growth, can be used to create a fantastic

Colorful foliage is a major component of modern planting designs

parasol of autumn tints that will win the admiration of any passerby. Since the best foliage color is usually produced on the fresh young growth following the removal of the growing tips, the number of flowers actually produced on a fuchsia grown for its foliage can be relatively small.

FUCHSIAS WITH ATTRACTIVE FOLIAGE

'Autumnale' Golden and coppery red.
'Colne Greybeard' Silvery gray-green.
'Firecracker' Dark olive green with cream variegation. Fresh growth tinged with pink.
F. magellanica **var.** *molinae* **'Sharpitor'** Lovely cream and green variegation.
F. magellanica **'Versicolor'** Variegated and tinged with pink.

'Genii' Glowing golden yellow leaves. Best grown in full sun.
'Ornamental Pearl' Greenish cream, tinged pink.
'Rosecroft Beauty' Green and cream with cerise shading.
'Strawberry Delight' Pale green and red-bronze.
'Sunray' Creamy green suffused with cerise.
'Tropic Sunset' Green and reddish bronze.

PLANNING COMBINATIONS

WHETHER THEY ARE GROWN in the open garden, in pots, or in hanging containers, fuchsias look well in the company of other plants. The variety of such plants is legion and choices will depend entirely upon individual preference. Many people would agree that the best arrangement is to have fuchsias as the dominant plant with the others complementing them.

GOOD COLOR COMBINATIONS

A great many fuchsia flowers have very strong colors; the bright reds, whites, and purples make it easy to plan a display of contrasting colors, but it is more usual to tone them down by using plants with more subtle or complementary hues. Many plants other than fuchsias are suitable for this purpose. Bear in mind, however, that pretty color combinations can be accomplished by using fuchsias entirely on their own; the strong reds and purples mix well with the pastel shades and the pure whites. Different fuchsia cultivars each have their own growth habits and optimum flowering times, which might cause the display to become slightly uneven. If this is unacceptable, plant groups of one cultivar together.

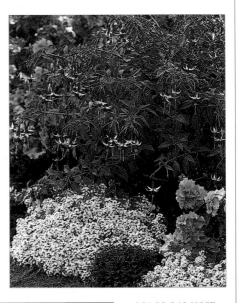

▲ COLOR BALANCE
The red and white of 'Checkerboard' is complemented by pinks and whites in this summer border.

◀ A COLORFUL FOIL
The green and white variegated leaves of F. magellanica *'Versicolor' contrast with the autumn foliage of* Berberis thunbergii.

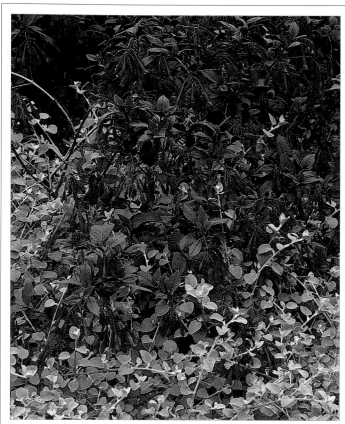

AN ENTRANCING
COMBINATION
*The bright flowers
of 'Gartenmeister
Bonstedt' stand
out against an
underplanting
of* Helichrysum
petiolare. *White
or pastel-colored
fuchsias can be
similarly enhanced
if they are planted
with strong-colored
flowers, such as
purple-flowered
verbenas.*

COMBINATIONS FOR CONTAINERS

For patio containers, height is often needed to give a display greater prominence. A fuchsia trained as a standard is one way to achieve this, although upright bedding plants, such as impatiens, begonias, or coleus, with their striking colors, also work well. These could even be planted around the base of a standard. The sharpness of the edges of containers can be softened by allowing cascading plants to flow over the edges; try lobelias, which are available in a range of colors.

Lobelias are also excellent in hanging containers; the blue-flowered *Lobelia richardsonii* looks splendid with red and white fuchsias. *Glechoma hederacea* 'Variegata', which has long, trailing stems and scented leaves, is another excellent companion of fuchsias for hanging containers; it will cascade straight downward and give the impression of great depth. Consider also verbenas with their bright flowers and weaving stems, *Bidens ferulifolia* to introduce a bit of that elusive

Strong colors are set off by pastel shades, whites, and silvers

yellow into the display, and any of the trailing foliage plants, such as the silver *Helichrysum petiolare* or the variegated ivies. Remember that some fuchsias, as in 'Autumnale', have attractive leaves, and these can be intermingled into your display.

FUCHSIAS FOR THE OPEN GARDEN

FUCHSIAS ARE ARGUABLY at their best when they grow in the shaded open garden. Planted permanently in beds made up completely of fuchsias or with other perennial plants, they repay a thousandfold the minimal effort required. Keep in mind, however, that fuchsias are hardy outdoors only in favorable parts of USDA Zones 8–10, with a few exceptions. In these areas, they thrive outdoors, but treat them as tender plants elsewhere, giving some form of winter protection – a deep mulch where they are marginally hardy; otherwise, overwinter them under cover.

WHICH FUCHSIAS ARE HARDY?

A fuchsia is considered to be hardy only if it can remain in the open garden throughout winter, even when the temperature falls below freezing. *F. magellanica* and its variants are the hardiest of all the fuchsias (hardy to USDA Zone 6 if given protection), and there is, fortunately, considerable choice in their flowers and foliage. In areas where fuchsias are marginally hardy, cold will probably kill the top growth, although new growth will emerge from the root system in the spring to form a new plant for that year (*see p.39*).

SEA SPRAY AND POLLUTION

Gardeners may wonder if fuchsias are tolerant of traffic pollution or the effects of salt spray in coastal gardens. Although it is true that some – perhaps the tender and pastel-shaded flowers – may be affected, most fuchsias seem to be quite happy living alongside a busy road or beside the sea. Most gardeners rapidly learn by trial and error which plants are badly affected by adverse conditions.

▼ HERBACEOUS BORDER COMPANIONS
Interplanted with shrubs of a similar height, fuchsias can be a permanent feature.

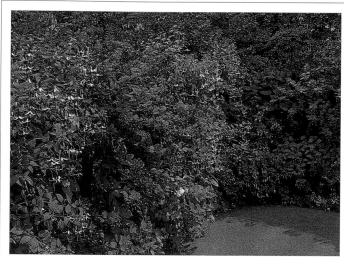

◀ FUCHSIA HEDGE
In mild areas, it is possible to use hardy fuchsias as hedges. Where marginally hardy, plants grown close together give extra protection to one another, so the top growth is more likely to survive.

▼ IN THE WOODS
Like other types of F. magellanica, white-flowered F. magellanica 'Alba' is quite hardy.

FUCHSIAS IN BORDERS

Any shady border is enlivened by the addition of fuchsias, with their enduring flower displays. Mass plantings of one cultivar can make a bold statement, but it is more common for them to be used as part of a mixed border with other shrubs, trees, and herbaceous perennials.

Bush fuchsias lend height and color to a mixed border and are usually planted near the middle; smaller annuals and perennials are placed near the front, and trees and taller shrubs go behind where they may provide light shade, which fuchsias love.

Fuchsias grown as standards, placed strategically around the border, can compensate for any lack of height. It is imperative, however, that standards are removed from the border and given protection before the onset of frost. Even if the standards are considered quite hardy, cold will kill the stem.

FUCHSIAS IN RAISED BEDS

The beauty of fuchsias is often seen to best effect when they are grown in raised beds. Trailing forms are particularly useful in this situation as the dangling stems relieve the starkness of the wall edges. Bush fuchsias will add height to the display.

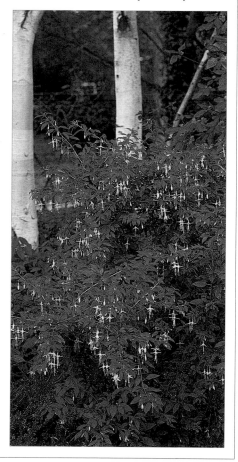

FUCHSIAS FOR SUMMER BEDDING

T HERE ARE MANY AREAS where fuchsias are not sufficiently hardy to endure winter if left outside. In such cases, fuchsias can simply be treated in the same way as other tender plants and given temporary protection during the cold months (*see p.39*). When the warm weather returns in spring, the fuchsias can be planted out in the open garden again.

COLOR AND HEIGHT

Fuchsias in summer bedding displays allow for considerable scope when it comes to color schemes, especially if they are co-ordinated with other plants (*see pp.16–17*). The inclusion of bush and standard fuchsias, perhaps of the more unusual cultivars such as the Triphyllas, brings height into the display, which is an all-important ingredient that bedding designs often lack. Not only does this present a very attractive display, but the fuchsias will also act as perfect foils for lower-growing

bedding plants, such as begonias or impatiens. A border edged with lobelias and alyssum serves to lead the eye inward to the coloring of the fuchsias.

HOW TO GROUP YOUR FUCHSIAS

Eye-catching displays are almost always the result of careful planning, and it pays to follow some key principles. The most fundamental of these is to position taller specimens at the back of the border to create a backdrop, which will emphasize those plants at the center of the display.

▲ OUT IN THE SUN
Unlike most fuchsias, those that belong to the Triphylla group tolerate a fair amount of direct sun.

▶ AN EXOTIC AURA
Any summer garden that has a border display full of fuchsias will have an unmistakably exotic atmosphere.

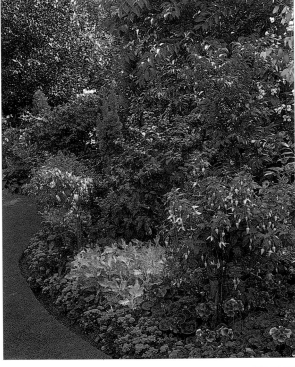

Further impact is made if fuchsias of the same cultivar are grouped together, preferably in threes or fives. You can make a formal bedding display even more striking by placing standard fuchsias around the border, but bear in mind that they need the support of strong stakes to prevent damage by gusts of wind.

LET THE ROOTS SPREAD OUT

There is always some debate as to whether or not fuchsias for summer bedding should be left in their pots when they are planted out. Removing the pots gives the roots plenty of room to develop and seek food and moisture, which results in larger flowering plants. The only problem comes when the plants need to be lifted in the autumn (*see p.39*), but the benefits of bigger plants with less anxiety over watering and feeding will more than compensate for this slight inconvenience.

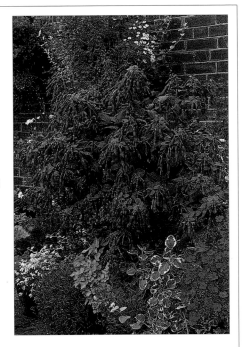

▲ BOLD COLORS
'Leverkusen', a bush Triphylla fuchsia, has intense flowers that contrast well with other bright colors.

◄ ADDED HEIGHT
The combination of bush and standard fuchsias in a summer border brings height into the display – an important ingredient for successful design.

FUCHSIAS FOR CONTAINERS

NO MATTER HOW LARGE or small a yard you may have, or even if you have no yard at all, it is always possible to enjoy growing fuchsias in containers. Fuchsias are perhaps the perfect plant for this type of display, and a visit to a garden center may open your eyes to the great choice of containers available. Let your imagination wander; old and unusual receptacles, like whiskey barrels or wheelbarrows, can all be used as containers to make attractive features.

THE USEFULNESS OF CONTAINERS

Perhaps the most useful feature of growing plants in containers is the flexibility. The positions of containers can be changed to present a different perspective, and when the winter sets in, fuchsias are easily moved to shelter where necessary.

Pots arranged on tiered staging can make a very decorative display, particularly when the plants are in full flower – all summer for some fuchsias. Ensure that containers are stable in windy conditions, however, since it would be a shame to see a well-grown plant rolling around on the ground with a smashed pot. Wrought iron stands that hold six or more containers are stable and attractive, and simple displays of grouped pots placed around on the patio are also appealing. Do not worry too much about the look of the pot – after all, it is not the pot that will eventually catch the eye but the cascading and beautiful effect of the plants within it.

A STANDARD AS A FOCAL POINT
For a point of focus on a patio, pot up a single standard fuchsia and underplant it with complementary flowers or foliage.

CONTAINER CULTIVARS

'Annabel' White flowers flushed with pink.
'Auntie Jinks' White and purple flowers.
'Blush of Dawn' White and pink flowers.
'Cascade' Pale pink and rich scarlet flowers.
'Dark Eyes' Red and violet-blue flowers.
'Eternal Flame' Salmon-pink and pink flowers.
'Glowing Embers' Pink and red flowers.
'Hula Girl' Deep rose-pink and white flowers.
'Kimberly' Pink and deep blue flowers.
'La Campanella' White and purple flowers.
'Marinka' Excellent red-flowered cultivar.
'Postiljon' White and rose-purple flowers.
'Quasar' White and rich violet flowers.
'Rosebud' White and rose-pink flowers.
'Salmon Cascade' Pink and orange-red flowers.
'Swingtime' Scarlet and pure white flowers.
'White Galore' White, fully double flowers.

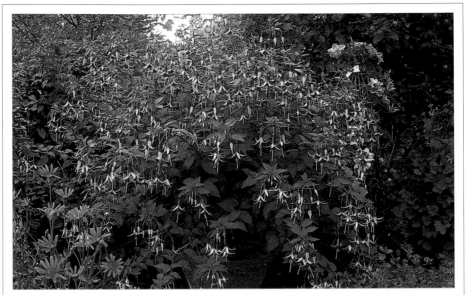

STANDARD FUCHSIAS IN POTS

Patios and other paved areas can benefit greatly from one or more standard fuchsias in pots, to relieve an appearance of flatness, and to gain height and visual interest. In its simplest form, one standard fuchsia is planted at the center of a container and surrounded at the base with either lower-growing or trailing fuchsias, or with other types of plants (*see pp.30–31*). Those specimens used to complement a standard fuchsia depend entirely on personal choice, but consideration should be given to the harmonizing of the colors (*see pp.16–17*).

Standard fuchsias are really quite easy to grow from a rooted cutting (*see p.47*). They do not require any special expertise; a standard fuchsia is simply a bush or trailing fuchsia that has been made to branch on the top of a tall stem, which you will first need to grow. If you prefer not to grow one yourself, some garden centers sell already trained standards, although they may be relatively expensive. A standard fuchsia with a clear stem between 18–30in (45–75cm) tall will probably serve you best. Always make sure that it is well supported with a strong, secure stake.

▲ OPPORTUNITY FOR COLOR
The bright blue flowers of Felicia amelloides *contrast perfectly with 'Checkerboard', which is grown here as a standard.*

▼ A MOVABLE FEAST FOR THE EYES
Pot-grown fuchsias thrive in a tranquil spot in the shade of a small tree during summer.

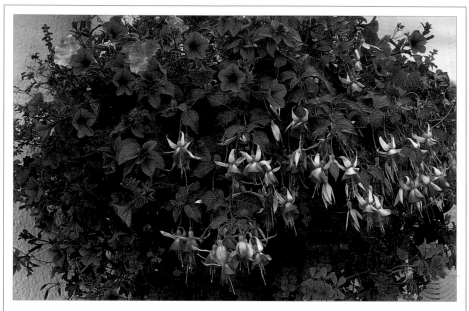

Fuchsias for Hanging Baskets

It is not necessary for hanging baskets to be made of wire mesh; any receptacle that can hold soil mix and has drainage holes will be satisfactory. Wooden containers, made to any shape or size you require, can be suspended from brackets so that your plants trail downward in an eye-catching display. Always consider carefully how containers are to be suspended; all brackets used should be securely mounted on the wall and of sufficient length and strength to support the full weight of the container when it is completely planted up.

Fuchsias for Windowboxes

Windowboxes can be used to great effect to display a colorful selection of fuchsias. Concentrate more on the lower-growing or smaller-flowered types, and allow the cascading stems of trailing fuchsias to spill over the edge. Try some of the dwarf fuchsia cultivars, such as these members of the 'Thumb' family: 'Tom Thumb' has red and purple flowers, those of 'Lady Thumb' are red and white, and those of 'Son of Thumb' are red and lilac. Since each of

▲ BUNDLES OF BLOOM
Do not worry too much about the look of the container – these fuchsias and petunias have completely enveloped their hanging basket in a mass of bloom.

▼ FUCHSIAS WITH FUCHSIAS
Here, bush fuchsia 'Tom Woods' is under-planted with 'Jack Shahan', a trailing cultivar.

◀ WINDOW DISPLAY
*Concentrate on
lower-growing or
trailing plants for
windowboxes so that
they do not prevent
light from coming
indoors.*

▼ A MIXED POT
*In this terracotta pot,
the upright and bushy
growth of 'Preston
Guild' mingles with
marguerites and
silvery* Helichrysum
petiolare.

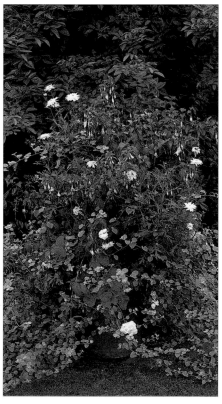

these plants grows only to a bushy height
of about 9in (23cm), they will not prevent
any light from passing through windows.
They all look good together.

FUCHSIAS FOR INDOOR DISPLAY
Fuchsias make extraordinarily fine indoor
table decorations, although they are not
really houseplants; they require a humidity

> For short spells only,
> fuchsias in containers
> make fine indoor displays

level that is not usually present indoors.
It is possible, however, to use fuchsias as
temporary visitors in the home if they are
placed in pots on a tray of permanently
moist pebbles, which will keep the air
reasonably humid.
 Fuchsias that have been raised as cuttings
on the windowsill, and have known no
conditions other than the dryness of a
house, may give quite satisfactory long-
term displays with minimum effort.

CARING FOR YOUR FUCHSIAS

CHOOSING AND BUYING FUCHSIAS

THE BEST TIME to buy young fuchsias for summer color is in early spring. Your local garden center should have some, and specialist fuchsia nurseries will be able to help with less common ones. The plants on sale will have been raised as cuttings the previous autumn and should be growing strongly. Examine each plant to make sure that there are no signs of any pests or diseases; look in particular at the stem and lower branches to check for any signs of mold.

SELECTING THE BEST PLANTS

Unless you intend to grow a standard fuchsia, choose a well-branched plant – one with the branches growing quite closely together. These fuchsias will produce the greatest density of flowers. If you see any young fuchsia plants in the nursery with tall, upright growth and plenty of distance between the leaf nodes, then these will be the easiest to train as standards.

BUYING TIPS
• Have a firm idea of how many plants you want to buy. It is easy to get carried away.
• If you intend to grow a standard, ensure the young plant has a strong, straight stem.
• Avoid plants that look overly large for the size of the pot.
• Select trailing cultivars for hanging baskets.

Closely branched growth produces the best flowers

Tall growth is easier to train into a standard

Flowers borne in leaf axils

Small fuchsias in trays are easy to carry

Clear label helps you choose the right type of fuchsia

WHAT TO BUY
Fuchsias are available to buy at different stages of development. Smaller plants are obviously easier to carry, although an older plant that has been trained to shape for you will save you the trouble at home. Also check the label to ensure that the fuchsia you want fits its future role in the garden.

◀ *F. MAGELLANICA VAR. GRACILIS Slim flowers are carried on strong, wiry growth.*

PLANTING OUT IN THE GARDEN

WELL-DRAINED SOIL and bright light to dappled shade from the sun are the main requirements of almost all cultivated fuchsias. The soil should be thoroughly prepared before planting, therefore, and a site that is in shade during all but early morning is ideal. Plant your young fuchsias, which should be growing strongly in their pots, only when all risk of frost has passed. Give any Species fuchsias as much uninterrupted root room as possible.

SOIL PREPARATION

It is important to prepare the ground thoroughly before you plant, since this is the way to get the best out of your fuchsias. First, clear the soil of persistent weeds by hand or with a suitable herbicide, then dig the soil over to the depth of one spade blade, forking in plenty of well-rotted organic matter as you go (*below*).

Finally, rake over the surface to break up any remaining clods of soil. In heavy clay soil, incorporate copious quantities of grit or compost to open the soil and improve aeration and drainage. Equally, light soil may need extra organic matter. Avoid digging when the ground is wet, because you may damage the soil structure.

ENRICH THE SOIL WITH ORGANIC MATTER
Unless your soil is already very rich, digging in plenty of organic matter will improve the soil's drainage, aeration, fertility, and moisture-holding properties, particularly if it is light and sandy. To avoid back strain, keep your back straight when digging, and take a break as soon as you start to feel tired.

THE BEST SOIL ADDITIVES

COMPOST
The contribution of organic matter to the productivity of the garden is enormous. It is easy to prepare from your garden and kitchen waste, which must first be allowed to rot down well. Compost improves the soil structure, adds some nutrients, and encourages the beneficial activity of earthworms.

WELL-ROTTED ANIMAL MANURE
Preferably with a high straw content, this serves the same purpose as compost. Avoid fresh manure, which may be toxic to plants.

LEAFMOLD
A fibrous and flaky soil improver derived from decomposed leaves.

WATER-RETAINING GRANULES
These granules are especially useful in soil that is prone to drying out. They hold many times their weight in water and are commonly used in container plantings.

GRIT OR GRAVEL
Improves drainage on heavy clay or compacted soils.

PLANTING OUTSIDE FOR SUMMER BEDDING

In frost-prone areas, tender fuchsias may be grown in the garden in summer as seasonal plants. It is possible to plant them in the ground still in their pots, which certainly makes life easier when they are lifted in autumn. If you do remove the plants from their pots, however, you will be rewarded with bigger, more freely flowering fuchsias.

Leave a distance of about 18in (45cm) between the plants if individual specimens are being used, or a distance of about 9in (23cm) between the plants if you prefer groups of three or four. The beds will fill out more quickly with closer planting, but the plants may crowd each other. Wider spacing will leave gaps for weeds.

1 Arrange the fuchsias into their display positions while they are still in their pots. Check the spacing (*above*), then water them well prior to planting.

2 Dig a hole for each plant, large enough to hold its pot. Place the plant in the hole, with or without its pot, and firm the soil. Add more soil to cover the root ball.

3 Water in well. Plants that have been left in their pots will need to be watered and fed individually throughout the summer, even if it has been raining (*see p.36*).

PLANTING HARDY FUCHSIAS

The best time to plant a hardy border is in spring, after all risk of frost has passed. Ensure that the soil is well prepared (*see facing page*) and the fuchsias to be planted are healthy, with moist soil mix. Because each plant's root system needs to be protected from winter cold, deep planting is essential. Make a saucer-shaped dip in the ground to a depth of 3in (8cm). In the center of the dip, dig a hole large enough to hold the plant's root ball, then place the plant in the hole so the top of the root ball is level with the bottom of the dip. Soil will naturally fill the dip over summer, and the plant will be at the correct depth in time for winter. Water regularly, feeding with a high-phosphorus fertilizer to encourage healthy roots.

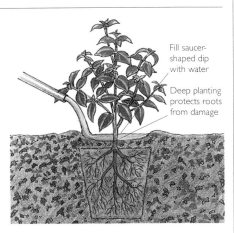

Fill saucer-shaped dip with water

Deep planting protects roots from damage

PLANTING FUCHSIAS IN CONTAINERS

FUCHSIAS IN CONTAINERS will give you a display throughout summer. Pots, windowboxes, and troughs are all ideal, although any sort of container can be used as long as it has drainage holes to prevent waterlogging. Raising the container slightly will also promote drainage. If the container will be in some sun, you should mix in some water-retaining granules. In larger containers where there is more soil surface exposed, pebbles and bark will help retain moisture.

YOU NEED:

TOOLS
• Trowel

MATERIALS
• Bucket
• Multipurpose soil mix
• Water-retaining granules
• Horticultural grit
• Classic planter, box, or barrel
• Stake and ties

PLANTS USED
• 'Paula Jane' (standard) x 1
• 'Barbara Windsor' x 4

PLANTING A CONTAINER

1 **Any good quality** soil mix will do. Mix in water-retaining granules, and grit to add weight, or the plants may topple in the wind.

2 **Partly fill** the bottom of the planter with soil mix and firm down gently. Do not overfill the planter at this stage.

3 **Remove the standard fuchsia** from its pot, and stand it on the soil mix in the planter. Gently tease out the roots, and ensure the stem is firmly staked up to the top.

4 **Position the pots** of the smaller fuchsias around the base of the standard. Assess how much space to allow, taking into account growing habit, such as trailing stems.

5 **Use a trowel** to completely fill the planter, around the empty pots in the top, with soil mix. Gently firm the soil mix, so that there are no air pockets, and fill in any gaps.

▼ THE COMPLETED PICTURE *'Paula Jane' is here trained as a standard, and used in this way it gives height and impact to the planting. Four plants of 'Barbara Windsor' – a bush – fill the corners.*

6 **Remove the pots** to leave a shape the exact size of the root ball of the smaller fuchsias, then drop these plants into their new holes. Fill with soil mix to just below the container edge. Water everything in well.

ADDITIONAL HINTS

• The use of a single fuchsia cultivar often works well in this kind of display.

• Add high-nitrogen fertilizer at the start of the season to boost foliage growth.

• Water-retaining granules mixed into the soil mix will help fuchsias in sunny sites.

• Frequent watering may leach out nutrients; restore with regular fertilizing (*see p.36*).

HANGING BASKETS

THE EARLIER IN THE SEASON that a basket can be filled, the better it will look. A basket made up in early spring will be well grown and ready for display as soon as summer begins. In cold areas, keep baskets in the greenhouse until all risk of frost has passed. A fully planted basket can be very heavy, so it is essential that any hardware from which a basket is hung is sufficiently secure. Also make sure that plants in the basket will not get damaged by being blown against a wall.

SINGLE AND MIXED PLANTINGS

Fuchsias look very effective in hanging baskets. A 14in (35cm) basket will hold five fuchsias from 3½in (9cm) pots: one in the center and four around the edge. An upright cultivar at the center will give extra height. The step-by-step guide on the following three pages shows how to plant a mixed basket; the procedure is the same for a single planting of fuchsias. Many experienced growers prefer to grow one fuchsia per 10in (25cm) pot.

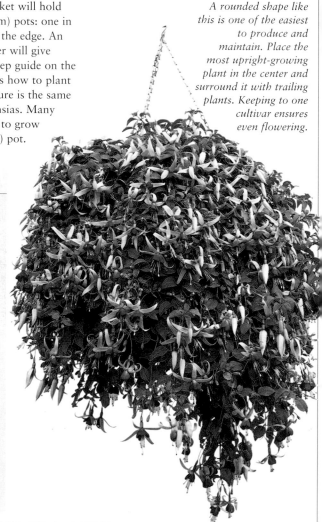

THE FINISHED BASKET
A rounded shape like this is one of the easiest to produce and maintain. Place the most upright-growing plant in the center and surround it with trailing plants. Keeping to one cultivar ensures even flowering.

SUITABLE PLANTS

'**Annabel**' Easily trained, versatile trailer with double flowers, rose-flushed white.

'**Auntie Jinks**' Trailer; free-flowering over a long season. Purple, white, and pink-red blooms.

'**Autumnale**' Grown for its colorful young leaves. Scarlet flowers.

'**Cascade**' Excellent in a basket. White-flushed sepals and deep rose corolla.

'**Frosted Flame**' Superb in a basket. Curling white sepals and flame red blooms.

'**Hidcote Beauty**' Creamy white sepals and pale pink corolla. Free flowering.

'**Marinka**' Vigorous, free flowering. Dark red blooms.

'**Peter Crooks**' Triphylla fuchsia bearing bunches of bright orange-red flowers at the ends of branches.

Planting a Mixed Hanging Basket

To get the most from your mixed hanging basket, aim to create an envelope of loose and trailing stems that will camouflage the container. Set trailing plants into the side of the basket (*see p.34, step 4*) as well as in the top. Use only young, healthy plants, and to retain the soil mix and hold moisture, make sure the basket is properly lined. Various liners are available, such as coir fiber, foam, and recycled paper.

You Need:

TOOLS
• Bucket or large flowerpot
• Scissors or craft knife
• Plastic bowl or bucket

MATERIALS
• 14in (35cm) wire hanging basket
• Coir fiber liner
• Soil mix
• Slow-release fertilizer
• Water-retaining granules
• Plastic

PLANTS USED
• Trailing lobelia × 2
• *Helichrysum petiolare* × 2
• Fuchsia × 2
• Ivy-leaved geranium × 2
• Trailing petunia × 2
• *Felicia amelloides* 'Variegata' × 1

Lining the Basket

1 **Place the basket** on a bucket or large flowerpot so that it is centered and level, to make it easier to fill and plant the basket. Fit the coir fiber liner, making several cuts, as shown, to ensure a snug fit.

2 **Press the coir** liner firmly against the bottom and sides of the basket, as it will be when filled with soil mix. Use scissors to trim off any liner that extends above the rim of the basket, to make a neat edge.

3 **Using a sharp** pair of scissors or a craft knife, make slits about 2in (5cm) long in the side of the liner for planting in tiers. Trailing plants inserted in slits at one or two levels below the surface of the basket will fill out and eventually conceal the wire frame.

PLANTING UP

1 **Empty the soil mix** into a plastic bowl or bucket and mix in slow-release fertilizer and water-retaining granules, according to the manufacturer's instructions.

2 **Add the prepared soil mix** to cover the bottom of the basket, filling up to the level of the first tier of slits cut in the side of the liner. Shake down the soil mix.

3 **To protect** the trailing plants that are to be inserted through the liner, wrap each in a piece of plastic to form a cone over the stems and leaves. (It is normally not necessary to plant trailing fuchsias in tiers like this, as their stems will naturally cascade over the edge of the container.)

4 **Insert trailing plants** – in this case lobelia and *Helichrysum petiolare* – through the slits made in the liner. Working from the inside, thread each plant through, carefully keeping the plastic cone in position to protect the stems and leaves. When the plant is in position, with the root ball on the inside of the liner and the leaves and stems on the outside, gently unwrap and remove the plastic cone.

5 **Continue to plant** the bottom tier. Gently tease out the root balls and add soil mix, working it around the roots and filling to within 2in (5cm) of the rim.

6 **Plant trailing plants** – here, fuchsias, geraniums, and petunias – around the rim, spaced so that they are not immediately above the plants in the lower tiers.

7 **Add more soil mix,** working it around the roots and firming gently. Leave a gap in the center for a bushy plant. *Felicia amelloides* 'Variegata', which is used in this planting, has blue daisylike flowers and variegated cream-splashed leaves.

FINISHING THE BASKET
Complete planting by filling up with soil mix so that the surface is about 1in (2.5cm) below the rim of the basket. Water thoroughly. Keep the soil mix moist while the plants become established, but do not overwater.

ROUTINE CARE

FUCHSIAS ARE NORMALLY forest-dwelling plants, so they thrive in conditions where there is bright light or dappled shade and reasonably high humidity. The soil around fuchsias should be kept fertile and just moist, and since most are intolerant of hard frost, you will need to offer them some kind of winter protection if you live in an area where frost is likely.

FEEDING AND WATERING

During the growing season, feed fuchsias regularly with a balanced fertilizer; it will ensure strong growth and profuse flowering. Guidelines may suggest a weekly feed, but many experts prefer to feed each time they water, using a solution diluted to about a quarter of the recommended strength. Apply plain water once a week if this method is used, to wash the soil of excessive nutrients.

WATERING A POT
Water can be applied either in the top of a pot or from below, in a saucer, but do not let the pot stand permanently in water.

Promote healthy growth by regular feeding

Water applied at the soil surface will seep down to the roots

Drainage holes let water out and air in

TIPS ON FEEDING

• Slow-release fertilizer mixed into the soil mix lasts for one to three months; after this, it is necessary to use liquid fertilizer.
• Allow a quarter of an hour for a potted fuchsia to soak up water from a saucer, then throw away any excess.
• Overfeeding will only damage fuchsias.
• Feed fuchsias grown for their attractive leaves with a high-nitrogen fertilizer.

RENEWING THE DISPLAY

Once the first flowers begin to appear in early summer, relax and enjoy the show; no more training or pinching out of the growing tips is needed. To maintain the quality of the bloom, however, regularly remove any flowers that are past their best; once berries begin to form, the flowering display may come to an early conclusion.

Many fuchsias with ornamental leaves produce their best coloring on very young growth, which can be encouraged by the continual pinching out of the growing tips. Any emergent shoots that have reverted back to their original all-green coloring must also be removed.

DEADHEADING
Regular removal of shriveled or damaged flowers will prolong the display and maintain its perfection.

SUMMER SHADING

During periods of hot weather, it is essential that you keep your fuchsias as cool as possible. In cooler climates, it will be sufficient to provide them with shade, but if they are growing under glass, it will be necessary either to move the plants outside or to provide special shading. An exception to the rule are the Triphylla fuchsias, which are able to take a little sun. Conversely, never put fuchsias in a position that is too dark.

HINTS ON SHADING

• Shade the glass in greenhouses either with blinds or shading compound, and regularly damp down the floors and staging.
• Aim to keep the temperature below 81°F (27°C), since many fuchsias tend to stop growing and flowering above this point.
• Positions not facing the midday sun are good, as are sites half-shaded by taller plants.
• Black pots are death traps in sun.

◀ SHADING IN THE GREENHOUSE
If you grow fuchsias in a greenhouse, they must be kept as cool as possible by shading the glass. Circulating fans will help to maintain an evenly low temperature.

▶ SHADING IN THE GARDEN
Partial shade is not only good for fuchsias, but it also suits a great many herbaceous perennials, so mixed plantings need not suffer. Make sure that any shaded area chosen for the display of fuchsias can easily be seen from the house or garden, and thin out old trees and shrubs if the shade created by them is too dense: heavy shade will seriously restrict growth.

REPOTTING A MATURE FUCHSIA

As a fuchsia begins to outgrow its pot, it will lose its vigor and start to show signs of poor health, such as yellowing leaves. When this happens, the time has come to repot it into a new container. Select a pot one size larger; go up in size by about 1in (2.5cm) each time to keep the plant in scale with the size of the pot. If a container of a similar size is chosen, then it may be necessary to trim the roots back a little. Make sure that the new pot is clean to avoid introducing pests or diseases.

1 **Check the soil mix** to determine whether it is necessary to repot. Compacted soil mix will no longer be free-draining or permeable to the air. Moss on the surface is a sure sign of sour soil.

2 **Ease the plant** gently from its pot and begin to crumble some of the soil away from the crowded roots.

3 **Free up** and tease out the roots. If the new pot is the same size as the old pot, it is advisable to cut back thick and gnarled roots by about one-third. Leave the thin fibrous roots intact.

4 **Put fresh soil mix** in the new pot and lower in the plant, then add more soil mix around the edges and firm in. For standards, add and tie in a new support stake. Water well.

5 **Trim back** the old top growth to encourage new flowering shoots. A severe pruning, leaving just one-third of the top growth, will revitalize an old plant.

OVERWINTERING INDOORS AND OUT

Potted fuchsias will come safely through a cold winter if two simple rules are obeyed: the plants should be kept frost free, and the root system should not be allowed to dry out. A garage or shed kept above freezing is adequate, especially if the pots are placed in a large, insulated box. Fuchsias survive in darkness for a few months, but trim the shoots back when the plants are brought out in spring. Hardy fuchsias remain outdoors; a thick layer of mulch spread around the roots will give protection.

TIPS ON OVERWINTERING

• After the first severe frost, do not remove the dead branches from hardy fuchsias. These branches will help protect the root system.

• Check regularly to ensure the soil around potted fuchsias is not allowed to dry out.

• If fuchsias are to keep growing, site them in a well-lit greenhouse at 41–45°F (5–7°C).

• If you are unsure about the hardiness of any fuchsias left outdoors, then take cuttings in the autumn and overwinter these indoors.

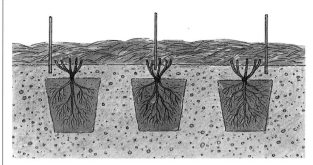

BURYING FUCHSIAS
This is a useful method where there is no room indoors for overwintering, and your winters are not severe. Dig a hole or trench deep enough to take the whole root ball and some of the stem. Fill the hole with garden soil, cover with straw, and mark the site.

PROMOTING SPRING GROWTH

Fuchsias flower only on the current season's new growth, so you need to encourage fresh growth by severe pruning. As the temperature rises in spring, new shoots will appear. If the winter has been very mild, shoots may appear from the old branches. It is important, however, to cut back most of the old wood, even if it is bearing shoots, in order to encourage strong fresh growth from ground level upward. Apply fertilizer to boost growth and encourage the regeneration of the plants.

PRUNING A STANDARD FUCHSIA
After a cold winter in an unheated greenhouse, the top growth has died back. Cut back old wood and allow the new growth to develop.

PRUNING A HARDY BUSH FUCHSIA
Leave the old growth until spring, then cut the old branches back to near ground level, even if new shoots are emerging higher up.

How to Propagate Fuchsias

GENERALLY, THERE ARE three types of propagation: seed, cuttings, and grafting. Grafting is little practiced, and seeds from cultivars are rarely as good as the parent plants, but a fuchsia cutting – a small piece of cut stem – will, when rooted, produce a plant that bears foliage and flowers identical to the plant from which it is taken. Even the most brown-thumbed of gardeners can root fuchsia cuttings successfully; the only requirements are moisture and warmth.

Taking Cuttings

In spring or late autumn, there is always a plentiful supply of potential cuttings on a fuchsia. First, choose a healthy, vigorous plant, then simply remove a section of stem. On the whole, it is best to use a sharp knife (it provides a clean cut), but your finger and thumb will do, even though this may cause bruising. A single stem can yield quite a number of cuttings if the three techniques shown below are combined.

TAKING A SOFT-TIP CUTTING
This is the easiest cutting to root. Sever the tip of a young branch just above the next set of leaves down the stem.

AN INTERNODAL CUTTING
Remove the soft tip, then cut just above the second set of leaves to give a pair of leaves between two pieces of stem.

A SINGLE-LEAF CUTTING
Cut the stem as for an internodal cutting. The cutting will then need to be sliced in half (see below).

A SOFT-TIP CUTTING
This cutting consists of a growing tip, an immature set of leaves, and a mature set.

TRIM THE LEAVES
With this internodal cutting, the leaves can be reduced in size to lessen water loss.

SLICING A SINGLE-LEAF CUTTING
Carefully slice along the stem between the leaves to make two single-leaf cuttings, each with a shoot growing in the leaf axil. Once planted, the shoot will grow into a new plant.

ROOTING CUTTINGS IN SOIL MIX

Fuchsia cuttings will root in almost any substance that retains moisture, including pure water, although the ideal soil mix seems to be an equal mixture of peat and vermiculite. This is an open and loose, low-nutrient medium that allows for the development of a healthy root system. With the use of a closed case to keep conditions warm and moist, your cuttings can be left to their own devices and will root in about two to three weeks.

PRACTICAL HINTS

• Any transparent container that can be sealed, such as a jelly jar or cut-down soda bottle, will be useful.
• Do not firm the soil mix – let it remain open and loose.
• Sharp sand is an alternative to vermiculite.
• Take care with heated closed cases as excessive warmth will kill the roots.
• Do not allow leaves of cuttings to overlap.

1 Make a small hole, then push the cuttings gently into the soil mix so that the leaves are just above the surface. If you are unsure about ease of rooting, begin by dipping the base of each stem in hormone rooting powder or liquid.

2 Continue to place the cuttings until all the cells in the strip have been filled. Instead of a cell pack, like the one shown on this page, you can fill a single pot with several cuttings.

3 Water the cuttings gently, then place them in a closed case or under a tented plastic bag (supported with stakes). Choose a cool position – about 61°F (16°C) should be sufficient – with shade from direct sun. No further action needs to be taken until new growth appears.

ROOTING CUTTINGS IN FLORISTS' FOAM

This method of propagation is a very simple way to root soft-tip cuttings. Florists' foam is used instead of soil mix, which makes it a neat job: something that can be done in the kitchen. The soft-tip cuttings are prepared in the normal way (*see p.40*) and allowed to root in the warm and humid atmosphere of a closed case. Only when they have rooted are they transferred to pots – still with the foam attached – where the plants will continue to grow.

PRACTICAL HINTS

• Take care not to crush the stems of the cuttings when handling. It is best to handle cuttings by their leaves.

• Fuchsia cuttings are susceptible to a range of pests and diseases, so take cuttings only from clean and healthy plants.

• When potting up, cover all the foam with soil mix. Exposed foam acts as a wick and draws moisture away from the roots.

1 **Cut a block** of florists' foam into 1in (2.5cm) cubes. Soak the cubes in water for 10–15 minutes, then place them in a saucer or tray. Use a knitting needle to make a ½in (1cm) deep hole in the center of each cube.

2 **Insert a cutting** into each cube. Cuttings should sit with the leaves just above the surface and the base touching the bottom of the hole. If the hole is too shallow, deepen it with the needle; do not push the cutting.

3 **Add water** to the saucer to a depth of about ½in (1cm). Label and place the cuttings in a closed case, or inside a plastic bag (tented with stakes), in bright indirect light at about 61°F (16°C), until rooted (*inset*).

4 **Pot up the cuttings** singly into 3in (8cm) pots of soil mix when their roots show through the foam. Cover the foam with ¼in (5mm) of soil mix to prevent the roots from drying out.

POTTING UP

Once the cuttings start to show healthy top growth, a root system has begun to form. This growth will develop into a strong, bushy fuchsia only if the rooted cuttings are moved to larger containers.

For the first few days, remove the lid of the closed case during daylight hours to accustom the rooted cuttings to a less humid atmosphere. Finally, remove the lid altogether, then pot each cutting into its own 3in (8cm) container. Place a small quantity of fresh soil mix (see *below*) in the base of the new pot, position the young plant inside with its roots spread out, and fill around the roots with more mix. Gently tap the filled pot on the bench to settle the mix. Do not firm by hand; subsequent waterings do this job naturally.

As the young plant continues to grow, it may be necessary to pot it on several times. To minimize root disturbance, use the technique shown on pp.30–31, steps 4–6, to mold shapes into fresh soil mix into which the root ball can be lifted.

POTTING ON

If left in a confined root space for too long, growth will slow down and may even stop. Giving fuchsias additional space for the roots to develop is therefore an essential part of cultivation; the usual advice is to pot on cuttings into pots approximately 1in (2.5cm) larger.

WHICH SOIL MIX TO USE

When faced with the considerable amount of choice available today, it is no wonder that newcomers get worried about which soil mix to use. In fact, there is no need to worry; fuchsias will grow well in virtually any type of soil mix, so long as it is moist but well drained (not wet) and well aerated. Avoid the temptation to use soil from the garden; it often gives disappointing results. Some mixes are improved by certain additives; you might find it useful, for example, to add water-retaining granules to the mix if the container is to be positioned in some sun. As for nutrients, the amount contained in a mix when it is purchased is of little importance, since fuchsias are fed from a relatively early age during watering (see p.36).

SOIL-BASED MIXES

These mixes provide ideal conditions for long-term growth. They are rich in organic matter, free draining, and their good structure ensures adequate aeration of the roots.

PEAT-BASED SOIL MIXES

Although these mixes dry out more quickly than soil-based ones and are prone to water-logging, peat-based mixes may be improved by the addition of grit (to give added weight and stability), and perlite or vermiculite (to improve drainage, provide aeration to the roots, and remoisten dry mixes). The quantity of these products to be added is not critical and can be based on the premise that if it feels right, then it probably is.

TRAINING INTO SHAPES

THE TRAINING OR SHAPING of a fuchsia can begin once the young cutting has developed a good root system: in fact, as soon as it is transferred into its first individual pot. For most, the same basic type of training is required, since the intention is to get bushy plants, but with the rapid and strong growth of most cultivars, it is easy to train them into a variety of shapes. Species fuchsias are the exception to this rule; most of them must be allowed to grow naturally.

SHAPES TO CHOOSE FROM

The natural desire of most fuchsias is to grow straight up along the central stem. If left to its own devices, this would produce a messy and unwieldy plant. The growth of a fuchsia, however, is easily manipulated; all that is needed to encourage bushiness, for example, is to remove the growing tip from the central stem, which will promote growth of sideshoots from the leaf axils.

This is called pinching. If even bushier plants are required, pinch the growing tips of each of the sideshoots as well (*see p.46*).

Standards (*see p.47*), espaliers (*see facing page*), columns, and pyramids are all relatively simple to train, but they need dedication, patience, and care, since it takes at least two years to achieve the shape required. In cold climates, therefore, winter

RECOMMENDED SHAPES
Since fuchsias have a strong and vigorous tendency to grow straight up, most cultivars can be manipulated to grow into any of the shapes shown here. Always start with a strong, upright-growing cultivar. From left to right is 'Mieke Meursing' trained as a bush, 'Celia Smedley' as a standard, 'Display' as an espalier, 'Flirtation Waltz' as a pyramid, and 'Mrs. Lovell Swisher' as a column.

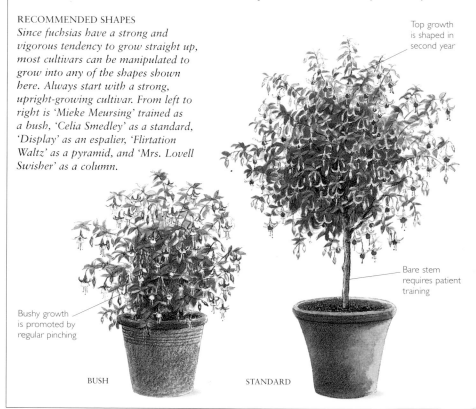

Top growth is shaped in second year

Bare stem requires patient training

Bushy growth is promoted by regular pinching

BUSH

STANDARD

protection in heated accommodation will be necessary (see p.39).

Miniature versions of these structures can be achieved more quickly, and they are normally grown in smaller containers to achieve a balanced look between pot and plant. Since fuchsias rapidly become woody when grown in small pots, they also make good bonsai plants. Select a cultivar such as 'Postiljon', with small flowers and foliage. Promote dense, bushy growth by continually pruning back during the first growing season; do the actual shaping during the second and third years.

Many fuchsias with thin, wiry growth (the Encliandra group in particular) can be used for topiary work. Trained around wire structures, they will quickly fill the desired shape and will produce a very pleasing effect with their flowers and foliage.

CREATING AN ESPALIER

An espalier is a plant trained with a vertical central stem and several tiers of branches growing horizontally on either side in a single plane. Fruit trees are commonly trained into espaliers, but the decorative, formal symmetry works just as well for fuchsias.

1 Take a strong, upright-growing bush fuchsia, and allow the sideshoots to develop.

2 Pinch out alternate sets of sideshoots, so that all of them grow along the same plane.

3 Train the sideshoots along a supporting frame so that they grow horizontally.

4 Pinch out the tip of the central stem once the structure has reached its desired height. Do the same with the sideshoots when they are sufficiently long; this also encourages the structure to fill out.

5 For a triangular espalier, like the one shown below, let the sideshoots at the bottom of the structure grow longer than the ones above.

Horizontal sideshoots grow in just two dimensions

Pinch growth at apex of structure

Two parallel central stems make a full structure

Pyramid shape needs very bushy growth

ESPALIER

PYRAMID

COLUMN

PINCH PRUNING FOR BUSH FUCHSIAS

Fuchsias that will be grown as bushes in pots, in hanging containers, or in the border all require the same type of training. The object is to create a well-branched plant, and the more branches a fuchsia has, the more flowers it will give.

To encourage the growth of sideshoots, the upward growth must be stopped, which is simply achieved by removing the growing tip from the main shoot. The energy of the plant will now be directed toward the buds, which are in each of the leaf axils on the stem. These will grow, and within about four weeks, each will have developed two or three sets of leaves with their own growing tips. The process can be repeated two or three times until the plant is sufficiently bushy; then allow it to mature and flower (*see below*). Bear in mind, however, that each pinching of the branches delays flowering.

As the plant matures, turn it regularly so that each side gets a fair share of light, which ensures even flowering. The use of a reflector box (a box lined with aluminum foil) is very convenient in the first days of spring if cuttings are kept on a windowsill.

1 **Remove the** growing tip of the main stem to promote growth of sideshoots.

2 **After a few weeks,** pinch out the growing tips of each new sideshoot to encourage more branching.

3 **Let the plant** mature after a final pinching out of the latest sideshoots. The first flowers should appear in about 8–10 weeks.

A FAN-TRAINED BUSH FUCHSIA
The growth of this bush fuchsia has been forced to branch out at an early age. Each branch has then been trained along a supporting stake to give its final shape.

TRAINING FUCHSIAS AS STANDARDS

To get a head start on training a standard, encourage autumn cuttings to grow steadily through winter by keeping them warm and well lit (*see p.39*). The greater part of the height will be achieved prior to rapid growth in spring. Choice of cultivar is not all that important, since any fuchsia can be trained as a standard, but select only cuttings that are growing straight up. A boost with balanced fertilizer ensures strong growth.

1 Pinch out any sideshoots as they appear in the leaf axils. Insert a stake and tie in the stem.

2 Keep removing sideshoots to make a tall, straight stem, but do not remove the stem leaves.

3 When the stem is 3 leaf sets taller than required, pinch out the tip. Repot and restake if necessary.

4 Pinch out the tips of the sideshoots at the top of the stem. Repeat until a round head is formed.

SUITABLE PLANTS

'Annabel' Makes a weeping standard with pale flowers.
'Barbara' Strong bushy growth; pale pink flowers.
'Border Queen' Great bush with two-toned flowers.
'Celia Smedley' Distinctive, easy-to-train bush.
'Checkerboard' Excellent bush; red and white flowers.
'Hawkshead' One of the best white-flowered bushes.
'La Campanella' Makes a floriferous weeping standard.
'Liebriez' Bush; good as a mini standard.
'Lindisfarne' Bush; good as a mini standard.
'Nellie Nuttall' Bush; easily trained into most shapes.
'Phyllis' Easy-to-train bush.
'Postiljon' Weeping standard.
'Thalia' A Triphylla bush with orange-scarlet flowers.

A FINISHED STANDARD
As soon as the head has bushed out, remove all the leaves on the tall stem. Keep the plant anchored to its stake, since this will give the stem greater strength.

PESTS AND DISEASES

LIKE SO MANY OTHER PLANTS, fuchsias are troubled by certain pests and diseases, some of which will cause serious damage if they are left untreated. As always, the prevention is better than the cure, although the methods of treatment are usually quite straightforward. With careful management and regular inspection of your plants, you can prevent pests and diseases from gaining the upper hand.

DIAGNOSIS AND TREATMENT

APHIDS AND WHITEFLIES

Aphids are unmistakable pests found around growing tips, sucking the sap from young plants to leave the growth distorted and stunted. The foliage may become yellow and drop off and a sticky honeydew remains, which looks unsightly, attracting ants and encouraging the growth of sooty mold. Whiteflies live on leaf undersides and appear in clouds when a heavily infested plant is disturbed. Spray with a strong jet of water, an insecticide, or a weak solution of dishwashing liquid. *Encarsia formosa*, a biological control, preys on whiteflies.

BLACK VINE WEEVILS

The larvae of this pest eat roots, causing sudden wilting. The most effective controls are to use a special soil mix containing a slow-release pesticide or to water pot plants with a pathogenic nematode in late summer.

BLACK VINE WEEVIL LARVAE
If a potted fuchsia wilts without warning, remove the pot and examine the roots. It is possible that you will find grubs like these.

FUCHSIA GALL MITES

These tiny mites cause new growth to swell and distort, forming galls. Leaf hairiness may increase, and leaves often turn reddish or silvery. In severe infestations, the plants stop blooming and abnormal growth appears on every branch. Destroy all growth showing symptoms; be sure to prune branches at least two nodes below the apparently infested area. Severe pruning in spring will eliminate many of the over-wintering mites and eggs. Spray with dormant oil in spring.

WHITEFLY TROUBLE
Whiteflies are easy to see when present in large numbers, such as on these heavily infested leaves.

GRAY MOLD (*BOTRYTIS*)

Browning then blackening of young stems, with furry gray mold, are the first signs of this disease. It usually arises as a result of neglect: careless watering, bad handling, or poor air flow. Treatment with fungicide is effective, although good ventilation will prevent the disease from occurring.

RUST

The early symptoms of rust are brown spots on the upper surface of the leaves, with pale orange pustules below. They look similar to rust found on metal, so the disease is well named. Remove infected leaves and spray with a fungicide, but take care; fuchsias are sensitive to some sprays.

SPIDER MITES

One of the worst fuchsia pests, these tiny mites usually appear on fuchsias grown under cover. Even though they are barely visible to the naked eye, the symptoms are clear: bronzed leaves, fine webbing, and eventual defoliation. The mites spread quickly and are treated by regular and thorough spraying with water or a miticide. *Phytoseiulus persimilis* is a biological control. Maintain humidity as a preventive measure.

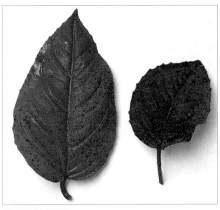

SOOTY MOLD
The honeydew deposited by aphids tends to be a breeding place for sooty mold fungus, which causes the leaves to discolor and die.

THRIPS

These tiny, slender insects suck sap and may be visible on flowers, particularly in hot weather, when they proliferate. Mist plants regularly to increase humidity under glass when temperatures are high, or use an appropriate insecticide.

DIAGNOSIS CHECKLIST

SYMPTOM	CAUSE
Falling and yellowing of leaves	Aphids
Stunted growth	Aphids
Distorted tips	Aphids
Sooty deposits of honeydew	Aphids or whiteflies
Plants collapsing	Black vine weevils (larvae)
Notches in leaf margins	Black vine weevils (adults)
Increased leaf hairiness	Fuchsia gall mites
Abnormally red leaves	Fuchsia gall mites
Silvery leaves	Fuchsia gall mites
Flowering stops	Fuchsia gall mites
Swollen and distorted new growth	Fuchsia gall mites
Furry gray mold	Gray mold (*Botrytis*)
Stems and shoots turning brown and black, often accompanied by furry gray mold	Gray mold (*Botrytis*)
Orange spots on leaves	Rust
Bronzing of foliage and leaf fall	Spider mites
Fine webbing between leaves	Spider mites
Silver spotting on foliage	Thrips
Silver spotting on flowers	Thrips

SEASONAL CALENDAR

SPRING

• To encourage new top growth on fuchsias, prune back old branches so that there are two or three old leaf joints with young buds awaiting development (*see p.39*).

• Repot fuchsias to stimulate root growth (*see p.38*). Remove as much of the old soil mix as possible, trim off any old and gnarled roots, and move the fuchsias into clean pots of a size that will comfortably take the new root ball (this is often the same size as the pots from which they were taken).

• Regularly spray the top branches with tepid water to soften the young buds and encourage new growth.

• Keep an eye open for pests and diseases, particularly aphids and fuchsia gall mites (*see pp.48–49*)

• Take small soft-tip cuttings when they become available. Have the shape of your new plants in mind as you take the cuttings (*see pp.40–41*).

• Keep cuttings at about 61°F (16°C) in a closed case (*see pp.41 and 42*). Spray regularly any cuttings in open conditions.

• When cuttings are well rooted, pot up each into its own 3in (8cm) container (*see p.43*).

• Start the training process (*see pp.44–47*). Select those cuttings you wish to use for bushes, baskets, or standards.

• As the new plants fill their pots, it will be necessary to pot them on into slightly larger containers (*see p.43*).

• Begin to give plants a balanced fertilizer in late spring (*see p.36*).

• Visit garden centers or specialized fuchsia nurseries if you wish to supplement your collection with new cultivars.

• Consider trying some of the species or Encliandra fuchsias.

• Keep plants in greenhouses shaded from strong sun, and open ventilators and doors whenever possible (*see p.37*).

• Cut back the previous year's growth on hardy fuchsias that have overwintered in the open garden. Do this as soon as strong new growth appears from the root system (*see p.39*).

• Make up hanging containers using fuchsia of a single cultivar, or a mixed planting with other trailing plants (*see pp.32–35*). Grow them outside, but only when the weather is favorable – be ready to take them under cover if late frosts are forecast.

• Once all risk of frost has passed, fuchsias may be planted outside in the border, and hanging containers can be placed in their final outdoor positions.

SUMMER

• Continue to fertilize plants growing in containers with a balanced fertilizer (*see p.36*).

• In periods of drought, regularly water the soil around your plants to keep the soil uniformly moist but not wet. The use of water-retaining granules in hanging baskets or patio barrels may be beneficial.

• Continue to pot on developing fuchsias so that their root systems are not restricted (*see p.43*).

• Continue to take cuttings (*see p.40*), but take care to keep them cool – about 61°F (16°C).

• The training process (pinching of growth tips) must stop in sufficient time for the plants to develop flower buds, taking about 8–10 weeks after the final pinch (*see pp.44–47*).

• Keep a very careful eye open for attacks by insects and diseases (*see p.48*).

• If insecticides are needed, read labels carefully before use.

• Support strong upward-growing branches with stakes, if necessary.

LOOK AFTER THE MAIN STEM
Encourage growth at the head of a standard by removing any shoots that develop from its bare stem during the growing season. Also make sure the stake is securely in place, since the main stem can easily snap.

SEASONAL CALENDAR

TIME TO PLANT UP A HANGING BASKET
Even though baskets will not be displayed in their final positions until all risk of frost has passed, they benefit from a head start by planting up in spring.

• Remove any spent flowers before they have the opportunity to develop into berries (*see p.36*). If berries are allowed to develop, then flower production may stop.
• Regularly water and fertilize fuchsias growing in the open garden during dry periods, especially fuchsias in the open garden that are in their first season (*see p.36*).
• Pay particular attention to the watering and fertilizing of fuchsias plunged outside in the open garden in their pots.

AUTUMN
• Continue to fertilize and water your fuchsias (*see p.36*).
• Remove any flowers past their best to encourage further development of flower buds (*see p.36*).
• Keep a careful eye on the weather forecast and be prepared to take under cover, or to protect, any plants that might be damaged by

frost. Pay special attention to both hanging containers and standards.
• Give consideration to the overwintering of those fuchsias that you wish to keep for the next growing season (*see p.39*).
• Apply a high-potassium fertilizer, such as tomato or rose fertilizer, to help the wood mature prior to overwintering.
• Take cuttings from plants growing outdoors as an insurance against possible losses (*see p.40*).
• Outside, leave hardy fuchsias unpruned, but add a mulch of some insulating material, such as bark chips or straw, around the crowns for winter protection (*see p.38*).

WINTER
• Make sure fuchsias that are to be kept through the winter are in a frost-free position. Do not let the root system dry out completely (*see p.39*).
• All standard fuchsias should be brought indoors for winter protection. Protect them in three places: the root system (cover the pots with any insulating material), the stem (enclose in a tree wrap), and the head (trim back slightly and cover with a good wrapping of row cover).
• Outdoors, check on hardy fuchsias regularly, and replace any mulch that has been scratched away by birds or other animals.
• Fuchsias that are overwintering in a heated greenhouse will require a temperature in the region of 41–45°F (5–7°C) to keep the leaves from dropping.
• For fuchsias under cover, water should be carefully applied, and only if necessary.
• On mild days, allow air to circulate through the greenhouse by opening vents and doors.
• Cuttings taken in autumn can be potted up once they are rooted (*see p.43*), but keep them warm and as close to the light as possible.

SOFT-TIP CUTTINGS
This is the easiest and quickest way to propagate fuchsias (see p.40). Cuttings can be taken almost all year, although the best time is autumn or spring. Remove them with a sharp knife from the shoot tips.

A GALLERY OF FUCHSIAS

THE FUCHSIAS DESCRIBED HERE are grouped into three divisions: the gallery begins with species fuchsias, followed by Triphyllas, and the final section is an A–Z of popular cultivars. Virtually all of these are hardy outdoors only in favorable parts of USDA Zones 8-10, although the hardiness limit can be stretched by providing ideal conditions and an appropriate winter mulch. Magellanica fuchsias can be successfully grown outdoors in Zone 6 with protection.

SPECIES FUCHSIAS

THESE ARE THE FUCHSIAS FOUND IN THE WILD and the ancestors of all the modern cultivated varieties. Over one hundred Species fuchsias have been identified, and both plants and individual flowers vary considerably in size, but the majority are distinguished by long, colorful tubes with trumpet-shaped flowers. Hummingbirds usually pollinate wild fuchsias, attracted by the bright colors and rich nectar, yet the flowers have virtually no scent. Although species fuchsias are often difficult to grow, requiring a lot of soil space for the roots to develop fully, they can be among the most rewarding of all fuchsias.

F. arborescens
Large clusters of small lilac blooms give this large shrub its name, the lilac fuchsia.

F. x bacillaris
An Encliandra fuchsia, with a bushy habit and distinctive small leaves and flowers.

F. cordifolia
A bushy fuchsia with slender, multicolored flowers against a background of broad leaves.

◄'AUNTIE JINKS' *A very free-flowering, trailing cultivar, excellent for hanging containers.*

F. boliviana
This unusual fuchsia can be
encouraged to climb. Allow
the roots to spread out fully.

F. boliviana var. *alba*
A climber, like *F. boliviana*,
but with white-tubed flowers.
Allow plenty of root space.

F. corymbiflora var. *alba*
A bush fuchsia with very
narrow flowers. The tubes
and sepals are pinkish white.

F. fulgens
A very vigorous, upright,
and bushy fuchsia. One of
the easiest species to grow.

F. hatsbachii
A good traditional-style
fuchsia, like F. magellanica.
The stems are wiry.

'Rubra Grandiflora'
This cultivar of F. fulgens
has upright and bushy growth.
It needs a large container.

F. hemsleyana
An upright-growing shrub,
with tiny flowers, growing
up to 30in (75cm) in the wild.

'Hinnerike'
A species hybrid with delicate
flowers. Pinch out new growth
to encourage a bushy shape.

'Loxensis'
A rampant, upright, and bushy
species hybrid. It forms a
good shape without training.

F. lycioides
Trailing, bushy growth with
fleshy leaves and small
flowers. Drought resistant.

F. magellanica var. gracilis
Upright and vigorous bush, with strong, wiry stems. The flowers are relatively small.

F. procumbens
Easy to grow with attractive, long creeping stems, and small, upward-looking flowers.

F. paniculata
A good species for the beginner, strong-growing and easy to train. Bushy growth.

F. magellanica
There are many cultivars of this species, like *F. magellanica* var. *molinae* 'Enstone' (*see p.69*).

F. simplicicaulis
An upright and quite vigorous bush that bears long-tubed, crimson flowers.

MORE SPECIES

F. excorticata Reaches a large size with care. Small, purplish flowers and unusual blue pollen.

F. glazioviana Strong and easy to grow. The small flowers have red sepals and violet corollas.

F. magellanica 'Versicolor' Upright with gray-green leaves, rose-tinted at first. Red and purple blooms.

F. venusta Strong, spreading bush. Red blooms slow to appear, but worth the wait.

TRIPHYLLA FUCHSIAS

'Billy Green'
A superb bush fuchsia with a profusion of flowers.

THIS EXCELLENT GROUP OF PLANTS is well worth growing. The flowers are distinguished by their particularly long tubes and trumpet-shaped sepals and corollas, and the blooms are generally held in large bunches at the ends of branches. The leaves are usually dark green in color, often with an attractive dark purple sheen underneath. Triphylla fuchsias are quite sensitive to cold, and so are best grown as summer plants, but with patience they may be trained as beautiful standards to provide added height and color to summer plantings.

'Coralle'
An upright and vigorous bush, with tapering flowers about 2½in (6cm) long.

'Edwin J. Goulding'
An excellent border addition, producing a profusion of red flowers throughout summer.

'Mary'
This eye-catching fuchsia has bright crimson flowers, and leaves with purple undersides.

'Peter Crooks'
A trailing bush suitable for hanging baskets. The flowers are produced in bunches.

'Stella Ann'
A vigorous, upright fuchsia. The foliage is olive-green with purple midribs, red beneath.

'Thalia'
A strong grower, but early training is recommended for a good shape.

POPULAR CULTIVARS

'André Le Nostre'
Introduced in 1909, this
strong bush is still popular.

WITH OVER TEN THOUSAND CULTIVARS to choose from, there must be a fuchsia for everyone, from classic single flowers to large and exuberant doubles, from purest white to red, pink, and purple. All are easy to grow and propagate, and they are ideal for summer color, whether grown in pots, on patios, in hanging containers, or planted permanently in the open garden. Marginally hardy varieties will, if protected, come safely through most winters. Your own experience is the best guide to determining the hardiness of a particular variety.

'Andrew Hadfield'
This very free-flowering bush
is good in a pot. The corolla
flares as the flower matures.

'Annabel'
A very versatile, trailing bush,
adaptable for bushes, baskets,
or standards. Easily trained.

'Atlantic Star'
The compact growth of this
single-flowered bush makes it
a good choice for containers.

'Aunt Juliana'
A trailing fuchsia good for
a hanging basket. It needs
support grown as a bush.

'Autumnale'
An attractive trailing fuchsia
for a hanging basket. Grown
for its colorful young leaves.

'Baby Pink'
A strong-growing double
fuchsia that makes an
excellent trailing plant.

'Ballet Girl'
A vigorous, bushy fuchsia
that makes a good standard.
It has fairly large blooms.

'Barbara'
A good bush fuchsia with
strong growth. Will also
train well as a standard.

'Bashful'
With its profusion of small
flowers, this bush is ideal for
long-lasting outdoor display.

'Beacon Rosa'
Medium-sized blooms on a
strong, upright fuchsia. The
corollas are lightly veined.

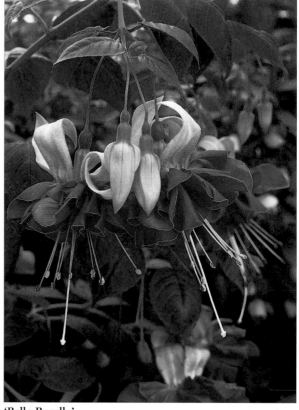

'Bicentennial'
A good trailer for a basket,
it will also train as an
impressive weeping standard.

'Bella Rosella'
This trailing fuchsia bears
very large, attractive double
blooms with magenta corollas.

'Blush of Dawn'
A highly recommended trailer
with large and long-lasting,
fully double flowers.

'Carmel Blue'
A particularly fine blue and
white bush cultivar that
produces flowers freely.

'Cascade'
A superb cultivar for basket
display, producing a tumble
of flowers. Serrated foliage.

'Celebration'
A trailer with marbled corollas and yellow-edged leaves. Suitable for a hanging basket.

'Celia Smedley'
An excellent, very vigorous bush with vivid flowers. Also good as a standard.

'Checkerboard'
This bush gives a succession of blooms through summer. An excellent beginner's cultivar.

'Dancing Flame'
A striking, double-flowered trailing cultivar. The large leaves have serrated edges.

'Deep Purple'
Vigorous and spreading, this double-flowered plant is good for a large hanging container.

'Dorothy'
Reportedly a bit hardier than many. Makes a showy hedge in favorable areas.

'Dusky Beauty'
This cultivar bears a
profusion of small flowers
on bushy, upright growth.

'Duchess of Albany'
Free-flowering bush cultivar.
Strong growing and suitable
for training as a standard.

'Eternal Flame'
The semidouble flowers stand
out attractively against the
dark foliage of this bush.

'Fiona'
This strong and spreading
trailer is excellent in a hanging
basket. Finely serrated leaves.

'Frank Unsworth'
The superb flowers contrast
well with the small dark
leaves of this trailing fuchsia.

'Garden News'
Good choice for the border.
The ruffled flowers are
borne on sturdy branches.

'Frosted Flame'
The long, barrel-shaped
flowers make this trailing
fuchsia ideal for a basket.

'Genii'
An upright bush with pretty
foliage and stems that redden
when grown in full sun.

'Glowing Embers'
Grown as either a bush or a
trailer, this fuchsia is very free
flowering with large blooms.

'Golden Marinka'
The variegated foliage is best
with sun. An early-flowering
trailer for a hanging basket.

'Grace Darling'
Bell-shaped blooms are
freely produced on this
bush with serrated leaves.

'Gretna Chase'
A free-flowering bush fuchsia,
with blooms of rose-pink and
white, and midgreen foliage.

'Gruss aus dem Bodethal'
This easy-to-grow bush
is famous for its striking,
very deeply colored corollas.

'Gwen Dodge'
A bush fuchsia that is very
free flowering. The blooms
are flared and look upward.

'Happy Wedding Day'
When open fully, this bush
bears very large, rounded
blooms. Needs support.

'Haute Cuisine'
Grown as a bush or trailer, this fuchsia bears large, deeply colored double blooms.

'Harry Gray'
Excellent in hanging baskets. Produces double blooms on short, trailing growth.

'Hermiena'
A self-branching trailer that flowers in profusion. Good for hanging baskets.

'Heidi Weiss'
An upright, self-branching bush with fully double blooms. The corollas have scarlet veining.

'Hidcote Beauty'
A trailing bush with strong growth that is well suited to a container.

'Jack Shahan'
Flowers over a long season.
Pinch the trailing stems to
maintain a good shape.

'Jim Coleman'
A strong, upright fuchsia
with semi-upright, bell-shaped
flowers produced freely.

'Jomam'
The slightly flared, bell-shaped
flowers of this bushy fuchsia
are borne in profusion.

'Joy Patmore'
A distinctively colored
fuchsia with green-tipped
sepals. Easily cultivated.

'Katrina Thompsen'
This is a superb, very
free-flowering bush. The
blooms are medium sized.

'Kegworth Carnival'
A good cultivar for a hanging basket. With support, it will grow as a bush.

'Komeet'
The corollas on this reliable, upright bush change to red-lilac as they mature.

'La Campanella'
A fine choice for a hanging basket, this trailing fuchsia develops rapidly once settled.

'Lady in Grey'
This double-flowered cultivar needs some sun. It is more difficult to grow than most.

'Lady Thumb'
Small foliage and flowers on a small plant – no more than 12in (30cm) tall and wide.

'Land van Beveren'
A trailing fuchsia with waxy white sepals that open to reveal a carmine-red corolla.

'Lena'
A highly versatile fuchsia that can be grown in a pot and trained into shapes.

'Leonora'
This bush fuchsia bears many soft pink flowers. The sepals are tipped with green.

'Little Ouse'
A large-flowered cultivar that may grow rapidly in a single season.

'Loeky'
This fuchsia with delightful flowers is suitable for training as a small standard.

'Love's Reward'
A superb fuchsia that gives great quantities of flowers through the season.

'Lye's Unique'
A very popular, free-flowering cultivar with distinctive white and salmon-orange flowers.

'Machu Picchu'
Regularly pinch the shoot tips of this free-flowering fuchsia for a good shape.

***F. magellanica* var. *molinae* 'Enstone'**
This bush fuchsia is valued for its green and gold foliage. The flowers are red and purple.

'Major Heaphy'
Keep the soil moist around this free-flowering, upright bush or the flowers will drop.

'Margaret Brown'
An excellent upright bush that flowers freely. Does well in the open garden.

'Margaret Pilkington'
The violet corollas of this fairly strong, upright bush mature to soft purple.

'Marinka'
A vigorous and very free-flowering bush that makes a superb hanging basket display.

'Micky Goult'
This fuchsia bears a profusion of compact flowers. It is useful in summer bedding.

'Mieke Meursing'
An upright bush with red-veined flowers. Cold drafts will mark the foliage.

'Minirose'
Ideal for smaller standards, this cultivar produces almost square-shaped flowers.

'Mission Bells'
Good for summer bedding, this is an upright, self-branching bush with serrated foliage.

'More Applause'
A trailer with large, fully double flowers framed by backward-curving sepals.

'Mrs. Lovell Swisher'
Small flowers are produced in great quantity on this vigorous, upright bush.

'Moonbeam'
An upright, self-branching cultivar with double blooms. It may need support.

'Mrs. Popple'
A bushy cultivar with vivid blooms among slender and serrated leaves.

'Nellie Nuttall'
This bush produces many small blooms through its long growing season.

'Orange Crush'
Striking salmon-orange blooms are borne on this free-flowering bush.

'Other Fellow'
Grown for its dainty, small flowers, this is an upright, self-branching bush.

'Paula Jane'
A free-flowering upright
bush. The deep purple
corollas mature to ruby red.

'Pink Bon Accorde'
An upright bush with small
to medium flowers, borne
slightly away from the foliage.

'Preston Guild'
This fuchsia bears plenty of
compact flowers. The sepals
flush pink when grown outside.

'Postiljon'
Vigorous and self-branching,
this is a good hanging basket
fuchsia with small flowers.

'President'
A fairly vigorous bush with
loosely formed, medium-
sized blooms.

'President Wilf Sharp'
A bush fuchsia that freely
bears medium-sized, double
blooms in shades of pink.

'Quasar'
The naturally trailing habit
of this cultivar makes it
useful for hanging containers.

'Rambling Rose'
Pinch out new shoots regularly
to produce a bushy trailing
plant for a hanging basket.

'Queen's Park'
An upright bush, valued for
its profusion of traditionally
colored flowers.

'Ridestar'
The flowers of this upright
and bushy cultivar show a
subtle combination of colors.

'Rose Lace'
Large, full blooms are
borne freely on this upright
bush with arching stems.

'Rose of Denmark'
An old cultivar, with green-tipped sepals on rather loose blooms. A bush or trailer.

'Rosy Frills'
A good hanging basket cultivar with a very free-flowering, trailing habit.

'Royal Velvet'
This vigorous bush has striking, richly colored, double flowers.

'Rufus'
A self-branching bush that produces flowers freely throughout the season.

'San Diego'
A good trailer for a hanging basket, with pinkish white sepals and rose-red corollas.

'Santa Cruz'
A very sturdy bush cultivar
with crimson blooms and
bronzed, serrated foliage.

'Sealand Prince'
An upright bush bearing
many medium-sized flowers
with narrow, upturned sepals.

'Sensation'
This trailer freely bears
huge flowers, which measure
over 13cm (5in) across.

'Snowcap'
This upright self-branching,
cultivar flowers profusely.
Train growth early to shape.

'So Big'
This pretty trailing fuchsia
for a hanging basket bears
double blooms.

'Swingtime'
A very vigorous trailer with
fluffy, fully double flowers.
An excellent basket fuchsia.

'Tom Thumb'
Small flowers and leaves on
an upright, self-branching,
free-flowering bush fuchsia.

'Tom West'
Grown for its variegated foliage,
which is encouraged by regular
pinching of the shoot tips.

'Walsingham'
This cultivar freely produces
semidouble blooms. The
corollas have crimped edges.

'Waveney Gem'
A free-flowering trailer
that will achieve an upright
shape if supported.

'Wedding Bells'
An almost pure white fuchsia.
The sepals are faintly pink
when mature. Bushy growth.

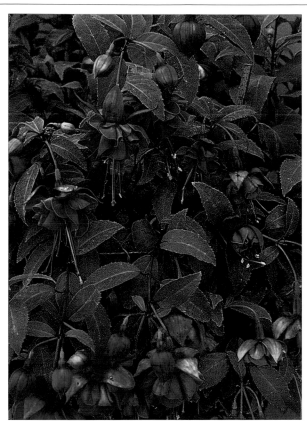

'Winston Churchill'
An excellent, self-branching, bushy cultivar, producing compact blooms in quantity.

'Yuletide'
A very showy bush cultivar. Very free flowering, on vigorous, upright branches.

MORE CHOICES

'Ann Howard Tripp' Very free-flowering bush; pink and white semidouble blooms.

'Bealings' Bush; bright violet corollas that mature to rose-pink, and white sepals.

'Bon Accorde' Bush good as a standard; white tubes and sepals, pale purple corollas.

'Centerpiece' Bush or trailer; fairly large, red and lavender semidouble blooms.

'Charming' Splendid bush; yellowish green leaves complement red blooms.

'Crackerjack' Trailing habit; pink-flushed white blooms, mauve-white at corolla bases.

'Dulcie Elizabeth' Bush; double flowers with pink sepals and rose-pink corollas.

'Gillian Althea' Bush; double flowers with pink sepals, and unusual, light blue corollas touched with orange.

'Hawkshead' Tall, strong bush; brilliant white flowers.

'Lakeland Princess' Upright and strong bush; red tubes; white sepals flushed with red; and violet corollas.

'Mayblossom' Trailing habit; small, white and rose-pink double flowers.

'Natasha Sinton' Trailer; pink and magenta double blooms.

'Olive Moon' Bush; semi-double blooms of pale pink and pale magenta.

'Rainbow' Strong, spreading trailer; red, dark pink, and violet double flowers with orange-red outer petals.

'Rosebud' Bushy habit, but needing support; white and rose-orange double blooms.

'Salmon Cascade' Trailer; pale pink sepals around deep orange-red corollas.

'Son of Thumb' Excellent low bush for a windowbox; cerise and lilac blooms.

'Wilson's Pearls' Trailer with red and white, semidouble blooms.

INDEX

Page numbers in *italics* refer to the illustrations.

ACKNOWLEDGMENTS

Picture research Cathie Arrington
Special photography Peter Anderson
Illustrations Gill Tomblin
Index Liz Granger

DK Publishing would like to thank:
All staff at the RHS, in particular Susanne Mitchell, Karen Wilson, and Barbara Haynes at Vincent Square; Fiona Wild for editorial assistance.

Photography
The publisher would also like to thank the following for their kind permission to reproduce their photographs:
(key: t=top, c=center, b=below, l=left, r=right)

George Bartlett: 53br, 54tl, 54bl, 54br, 55tl, 55tr, 55cr, 55bl, 55bc, 55br, 56tr, 56bl, 56bc, 57c, 57bl, 57bc, 58tl, 58br, 59tr, 59cr, 59bc, 59br, 60cl, 60bl, 60br, 61cl, 61bl, 62cr, 62br, 63bl, 64tr, 65tr, 65cr, 65bl, 66br, 68tl, 68cl, 68bl, 69tr, 69bl, 69br, 70tr, 70br, 71bc, 72tl, 73tl, 73cl, 73br, 76cr, 76br, 77t
Garden Matters: 8br

Garden Picture Library: Lynn Brotchie 37b; Chris Burrows 13bc, 15c; Eric Crichton 5bl, 14; Ron Evans 4br, 20l; John Glover 18, 19t; Sunniva Harte 8t, 9, 52; Lamontagne 25t; Marie O'Hara 23b; Howard Rice 2; J.S. Sira 8bl; Didier Willery 19b
John Glover: back cover tr and c, 13cr, 13bl, 20r, 21t
Harpur Garden Library: 16c, 21b
Andrew Lawson: 13c, 13br, 23t, 24b, 26
S&O Matthews Photography: 7, 17, 24t
Clive Nichols Garden Pictures: 6, 10bc, 12cr; Lower House Farm, Gwent 16b; Old Rectory, Berkshire 25b
Harry Smith Collection: front cover r, 10bl, 10r, 11t, 11bl, 11br, 12bl, 12bc, 12br, 13cl, 15t, 70bl

American Horticultural Society
Visit AHS at www.ahs.org or call them at 1-800-777-7931 ext.10. Membership benefits include *The American Gardener* magazine, free admission to flower shows, the free seed exchange, book services, and the Gardener's Information Service.